S0-BYV-374

IMAGES
of America

DOUGLAS

Donald Douglas (6 April 1892 – 1 February 1981) in the final assembly area at the Santa Monica, California, plant.

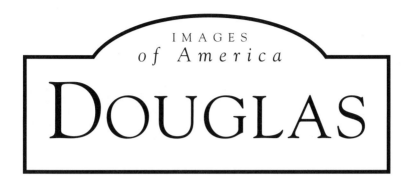

IMAGES
of America

DOUGLAS

Compiled by
Martin W. Bowman

TEMPUS

First published 1999
Copyright © Martin W. Bowman, 1999

Tempus Publishing Limited
The Mill, Brimscombe Port,
Stroud, Gloucestershire, GL5 2QG

ISBN 0 7524 1615 4

Typesetting and origination by
Tempus Publishing Limited
Printed in Great Britain by
Midway Clark Printing, Wiltshire

A KLM pilot and crew in front of their DC-2, one of 198 built. KLM was a long and valued customer of Douglas and was the first European airline to operate the DC-3. On 3 April 1961 KLM brought the DC-8 Series 50 into service.

Contents

Some 10,654 DC-3 and derivative transports were built by Douglas, plus 2,500 under licence, making it the most successful transport of all time. C-47s served in the Second World War, Korea and Vietnam, and hundreds were still flying as late as 1970.

Acknowledgements

The author would like to thank: Ashley Annis; Mike Bailey; the late Roland H. Baker; Roy Brookes; Nigel Buswell; Tony Carlisle; Mike Cleary; Mike Henry; Tony Hudson; Jake Krause; Paul Lincoln; Jerry C. Scutts; Graham Simons; Peter C. Smith; Paul Wilson; and the dedicated staff of the US 2nd Air Division Memorial Library in Norwich: Derek S. Hills, Trust Librarian; Lesley Fleetwood and Christine Snowden, all of whom were most helpful and who provided much willing assistance with research.

Introduction

Every young boy can dream! For Donald Wills Douglas, born on 6 April 1892, the son of Bill and Dorothy Douglas of Brooklyn, New York, his first love was ships. Eventually this fascination led him and his older brother to enlist in the US Naval Academy in 1910, but Douglas resigned after just two years to pursue an interest in aeronautical engineering. He finished the four-year course in half the time and in 1915 went to work for the Glenn Martin Company in California. During his five years with the company, Douglas served as chief designer on the MB-1 project, the Army's first bomber. In April 1920 he left to start his own aeroplane company in Los Angeles, where he teamed up with David Davis, a well-heeled Southern Californian who wanted to sponsor the first-ever non-stop, coast-to-coast flight. A Davis-Douglas Company was formed to design and build such an aircraft, which became known as the Cloudster.

This flew for the first time on 24 February 1921 at March Field near Riverside and, despite almost writing it off on the first attempt, Eric Springer got the Cloudster up at the second attempt and remained airborne for almost an hour. On 27 June the Cloudster took off for New York on the non-stop, coast-to-coast attempt but the flight ended abruptly over Texas when engine failure forced a landing at Fort Bliss, El Paso. Two years later, on 2 May 1923, two Army pilots in a Fokker took off from New York and landed at San Diego to snatch the transcontinental record. Davis sold his interest, leaving Donald Douglas to build up his company alone.

His first customer was the US Navy who, in 1922, ordered forty military versions of the Cloudster for torpedo-bombing, under the designation DT-2. Altogether, Douglas built forty-six DT-1s and -2s, including five for Norway and Peru, and another forty-four were built by the Navy and contract manufacturers. Encouraged, the US Army Air Service and US Post Office Department ordered derivatives of the Cloudster as O-2 observation and M-1 mail planes, respectively. The Army also purchased five DT-2s as Douglas World Cruisers, with interchangeable wheel and float landing gears, for the first round-the-world flight by aircraft of any nation. On 17 March 1924 four of the DWCs left Clover Field at Santa Monica, adjacent to the Douglas factory, and headed for Alaska. DWC *Seattle* was lost at Dutch Harbor in the Aleutians, *Boston* was lost in the North Atlantic, but *Chicago* and *New Orleans* arrived back at Clover Field on 23 September, returning to Seattle five days later. Staging through the Aleutians, Japan, India, Europe, Iceland, Greenland and the USA, they had circled the globe on a 27,534-mile journey in just over 371 hours of actual flying time.

In the summer of 1922 Donald Douglas took out a lease on abandoned buildings of the Herrman Film Corporation at 2435 Wiltshire Boulevard, Santa Monica, with an adjacent field available for flying, where, for the next seven years, he built many famous aircraft, including the Douglas World Cruisers. In 1929 Douglas Aircraft moved to a new plant on a $7\frac{3}{4}$ acre site next to Clover Field.

In 1931 Douglas bought just over a half share in Jack Northrop's El Segundo operation south of Santa Monica and set about redesigning that company's A-17 (Model 8) attack bomber (35-54 pictured at Mitchell Field in 1938) for the overseas market. Douglas built 351 A-17-8As.

When America entered the Second World War its carrier-borne scout and bomber squadrons were equipped with the SBD-2 Dauntless dive-bomber. At the time of Pearl Harbor it had been considered obsolete but the prolonged development of its intended successor, the Curtiss SB2C, which did not finally enter service until the end of 1943, saw the Dauntless fulfil a long and successful career, unsurpassed by any other dive-bomber in the world. Douglas built 5,938 SBD and A-24 versions.

The successful outcome of the first round-the-world flight brought huge orders for Douglas, including an order from the Army for twenty-seven of the passenger transport version of the DWC, known as the C-1. In 1929 Douglas branched out into commercial amphibians but the Wall Street Crash and the resulting depression led to most of the fifty-eight Dolphin production models (and the Sinbad prototype) being bought for the Army Air Corps, the Navy and the Coast Guard. In 1930 the Army bought seven Douglas gull-wing B-7 bombers and five O-35 observation versions. A year later, Donald Douglas showed an interest in John K. 'Jack' Northrop's El Segundo operation south of Santa Monica and in January 1932 bought just over a half share in the business to create the Northrop Corporation as a partially-owned subsidiary of the Douglas Aircraft Company. Douglas redesigned that company's A-17 (Model 8) attack bomber for the overseas market and in 1939-40 sold seventy-four Douglas 8-As to Sweden, Argentina, Peru, Holland and Iraq.

In 1936 project engineer Ed Heinemann began the development of another of Jack Northrop's significant pre-war creations, the twin-engined DB-7 attack aircraft. (A total of 7,098 Bostons were built by Douglas between 1939-1944.) Heinemann had joined Jack Northrop in 1932 and in 1936 became chief engineer of the El Segundo Division of Douglas. Northrop became general manager and chief engineer of the Douglas bomber programme before leaving to form a new independent company in 1939, but Heinemann was to remain with Douglas until 1960. In that time he became the greatest aircraft designer in the company's history, designing all its major combat aircraft during the Second World War and the post-war years.

Douglas' 1936 bomber design, the massive XLRB-2/B-19, with a wingspan double that of the B-17, never entered production, but in August 1934 the AAC invited US manufacturers to design a new, multi-engined strategic bomber. Boeing weighed in with its

Boston IIIs of 107 Squadron, No.2 Group, at RAF Great Massingham, Norfolk, on 8 April 1942. Bostons of Nos107, 88 and 226 Squadrons flew near-suicidal, daylight, high-level, pinpoint-bombing operations before transferring to 2nd Tactical Air Force in 1944 for pre-D-Day missions.

four-engined Model 299, later to become famous as the B-17, while Douglas and Martin went for the tried and tested route with twin-engined designs, the DB-1, based on the DC-2 airliner, and the Model 146, a B-10 derivative. On 30 October 1935 the Model 299 crashed following take-off with the controls inadvertently locked. Before the crash, the US Army had been considering an order for sixty-five B-17s but on 17 January 1936 production contracts were instead awarded to Douglas for 131 twin-engined B-18 Bolos (the DB-1 was less than half the price of the Model 299), while Boeing received only a service-test order for just thirteen B-299Bs and a static-test model. An additional 177 DB-2/B-18As were contracted in June 1937. In 1938 Douglas received a final order for another forty examples. Changes to the basic B-18 airframe were many and these led to a new version, the B-23 Dragon, which had a new and better-streamlined fuselage, a large fin and rudder and the DC-3's stronger wings. Thirty-eight Dragons were ordered in 1939.

The Douglas bombers were soon eclipsed by the Boeing versions B-17E and onwards. Performance was poor compared to the B-25 Mitchell and B-26 Marauder and by the start of the Second World War both the B-18 and B-23 had been rendered obsolete. However, the Bolo, in particular, had been available in numbers at a crucial time and thousands of much needed air crews were therefore available to make the transition to the B-17s then coming into service. (During the Second World War Douglas would be called upon to build B-17s.)

The Douglas Company was very successful in the pre-war commercial transport market, which began with a request from TWA that led to the design of the DC-1. In 1934 the first fifty-nine DC-2 airliners were built and in 1935 another fifty-three examples followed. A request from American Airlines led, in 1935, to the DST (Douglas Sleeper Transport), the

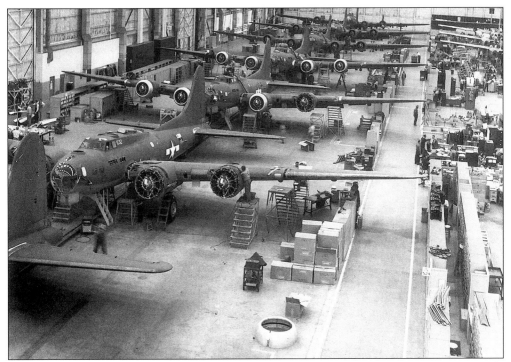

From 1 July 1940 to 31 August 1945 the six Douglas plants between them built 30,980 aircraft. Long Beach built the most (9,439), including over 5,000 C-47s, A-20 and A-26 (B-26) attack bombers, 605 B-17Fs and 2,395 B-17Gs (pictured), while Santa Monica turned out 7,309 A-20s, C-54s, C-47s and other DC-3 variants.

first model of the soon-to-be-famous DC-3 day-transport version. First flown on 17 December 1935, the first DST was followed by only thirty-seven more sleeper transports but by the late 1930s every major airline in the United States, as well as eighteen overseas airlines, were operating DC-2s and DC-3s. In November 1941 the Douglas Long Beach plant was opened for business; the first aircraft to be assembled there was a C-47, the military version of the pre-war DC-3 airliner.

Of all the Douglas plants, Long Beach built the most aircraft (9,439) during the Second World War. It produced over 5,000 C-47s and A-20/A-26 (B-26) attack bombers and 3,000 B-17Gs. El Segundo, meanwhile, turned out 5,938 SBDs and A-24 Dauntlesses, Chicago built 629 C-54 Skymasters, Oklahoma City built 5,319 aircraft (mainly C-47s and C-117s), Tulsa built 962 B-24 Liberators and A-26/A-24 twin-engine and single-engine attack bombers, and the main plant at Santa Monica built 7,309 A-20s, C-54s, C-47s and other DC-3 variants. From 1 July 1940 to 31 August 1945, Douglas built 30,980 aircraft, second only to North American, which produced just over 41,000 aircraft. Douglas had become the prime producer of transports for the allied air forces and the C-47 was the most numerous. Eventually, 10,654 DC-3 and derivative transports were built by Douglas (plus 2,500 under licence), making it the most successful transport of all time. Hundreds were still going strong as late as 1970.

After VJ-Day, August 1945, the leases on the plants at Chicago, Oklahoma City and Tulsa were allowed to expire after all their production orders were cancelled by the US government. While the world's major airlines looked to the US to rebuild their passenger fleets, substantial numbers of surplus military C-47s and C-54s flooded onto the market and companies like Douglas and its main rival, Lockheed, had to fight hard to remain

The D-558-II Skyrocket research aircraft, one of three built and the first aircraft to exceed Mach 2, air-launched from P2B-1S (B-29) on 4 February 1951.

competitive. The Lockheed Constellation entered service with Pan American Airways and TWA in 1946 while Douglas' DC-4 design was sponsored by American, Eastern and United Airlines. However, the DC-4, unlike the Constellation, did not have a pressurised cabin and was not as fast, nor could it carry as much payload. American and United therefore looked to the DC-6 to compete with TWA's Constellations. They began receiving the first models on 24 November 1946 and the DC-6 entered fleet operation with both these airlines on 27 April 1947. All DC-6s were withdrawn from service in November following two accidents but they recommenced operations on 21 March 1948 after a modification to prevent fuel overflow being sucked into a cabin heater duct (the cause of the two accidents). Despite this setback, the DC-6 proved very successful, some 704 being built, and it emerged as the most economical of all piston-powered airliners of the period.

Throughout the late 1940s and 1950s, Douglas, first with its DC-6, -6A, and -6B designs, and Lockheed, initially with its Constellation and then with its Super Constellation designs, fought a battle for pre-eminence in the four-engined turboprop commercial transport market. Interest from American Airlines led to the development of the DC-7, and the DC-7B and -7C models followed. The DC-7 began service with American Airlines on 4 November 1953 and the DC-7C entered scheduled service with PanAm on 18 April 1956. By late 1958 Douglas had produced 1,042 DC-6 and DC-7 series aircraft, including C-118 and R6D military transport versions.

Meanwhile, the Boeing 707, America's first commercial jet, flew for the first time in 1954, signalling the beginning of the end of the turboprop era. Douglas belatedly tried to catch up with its new rival, announcing on 7 June 1955 that it was entering the long-range jet transport field with the not dissimilar DC-8. This turbojet-powered airliner first flew on 30 May 1958, too late to mount a serious challenge to the Boeing 707. Development also suffered when it failed to achieve its guaranteed range (the same problem that was affecting

Conceived during the Second World War, the AD (A-1) Skyraider entered service in 1946, fighting in Korea with the USMC and USN (these AD-4Bs of VA-115 aboard the *Philippine Sea* are being armed for raids on the North Korean mainland in 1951) and serving the USN and USAF in Vietnam. No less than twenty-two versions were built, totalling 3,180 aircraft.

the Boeing 707), and Douglas had to dig deep to redress the situation. As a result, sales of the DC-8 went from bad to worse, dropping from seventy-three in 1955 to eleven in 1958. In 1959, the year when the DC-8 entered service simultaneously with Delta and United Air Lines (on 18 September), sales numbered eighteen and in 1960 only three were ordered. The DC-8 Series 50, which first flew on 20 December1960, was the first DC-8 to be powered by turbo fan engines instead of turbo jets, and entered service with KLM on 3 April 1961. A total of 88 DC-8-50s was built, and these were followed by three sub-series within the 'Super Sixty Series.'

Meanwhile, Douglas was heavily committed to providing military aircraft, such as the AD Skyraider, F3D Skynight, B-26 bomber (formerly A-26), and C-47 and C-54 transports, to meet the demands of the war in Korea. The worsening Cold War situation meant further orders were received for the A3D Skywarrior, F4D Skyray, C-124 Globemaster and new aircraft like the B-66 Destroyer, A4D Skyhawk and Boeing B-47. To meet these demands, production was increased substantially at the Santa Monica factory where the C-118s were produced, at the Long Beach plant where B-66s and C-124s were under construction and at El Segundo, where F3D Skynights, F4D Skyrays, AD Skyraiders, and A-4 Skyhawks were being produced. The government-owned factory at Tulsa, Oklahoma, was re-opened for Douglas to build B-66s and B-47s for the Air Force.

As a direct result, employment – and profits – rose dramatically during the turbulent 1950s, with net sales reaching an all-time high in 1958. However, one by one, production orders for many of these aircraft dried up. Between October 1953 and January 1961, the F3D, AD Skyraider, F4D and A3D all went out of production. In 1962 Douglas was forced to transfer Skyhawk production to the Long Beach plant. The company's failure to win large replacement orders for new military types including the XA4D-1, F5D-1 Skylancer (only four prototypes being built) and F6D-1 Misseleer (which was cancelled before the

A DC-6 of BIAS and a KLM DC-8 on a rainy night at Schiphol, Amsterdam. The DC-6 entered fleet operation with both American and United Air Lines on 27 April 1947 and eventually some 704 were built. The DC-8 first flew on 30 May 1958, too late to mount a serious challenge to the market leader, Boeing's 707, America's first commercial jet. When production stopped in May 1972, 556 DC-8s had been built.

prototype stage), coupled with its late entry into the commercial jet market, contributed greatly to its downfall.

The years 1959-1960 resulted in heavy losses and, though Douglas returned to profitability in 1961, the signs were that its airliner manufacturing business was in decline. By the end of that year, while 176 DC-8s had been sold, Boeing had raced ahead, selling 320 707s and 720s. Unable to fund development of other commercial jetliners and conscious that Boeing was working on a smaller medium-range jet transport (the 727), Douglas signed an agreement with Sud Aviation of France to sell and support Caravelle twin-jet transports on a world-wide basis. However, in June 1962 TWA cancelled its option for 40 Caravelles and ordered more 727s instead. Douglas' partnership with Sud Aviation collapsed and the company looked to a new short-range design, the twin-jet DC-9. This was actually smaller than either the DC-8 or the DC-7 and was built to compete with the BAC One-Eleven. Fifteen DC-9s were ordered by Delta in May 1962 but only fifty-eight had been sold by the time the airliner made its first flight on 25 February 1965. Despite this poor start, the DC-9 became the most successful of the Douglas Commercial aircraft, with 831 sold to airlines and 45 more built for the military market. Although the Boeing 737 ultimately outstripped sales of the DC-9, the follow-on Series 80/MD-80 was to prove equally successful. It would not, however, be built solely by Douglas.

By 1965 Douglas was building DC-8s and DC-9s, A-4 Skyhawks and missile and space products. Further diversification was catastrophically nipped in the bud by three hammer-blows. Firstly, its winning MOL (Manned Orbiting Laboratory) design was abruptly cancelled by the Department of Defense because of the need to re-allocate funds for the war in South-east Asia. Douglas then lost the contract to build the huge C-5A military

The B-66, of which 294 were built, was originally conceived in the early 1950s as a tactical light bomber and reconnaissance aircraft but evolved as a powerful ECM aircraft, RB-66C-DT (pictured).

cargo aircraft to Lockheed, while in the commercial sector the Boeing 747 effectively ended any hopes Douglas might have had with its projected double-deck, 650-seat transport aircraft.

By December 1966 it was obvious that the only way Douglas could raise sufficient working capital to remain competitive was to find a suitable buyer who was prepared to merge with the ailing Santa Monica company. On 13 January 1967 an offer by McDonnell Aircraft Corporation, which was headed by founder James Smith McDonnell as Chairman and Chief Executive Officer with David S. Lewis as President and Director, was accepted. On 28 April the McDonnell Douglas Company came into existence with Lewis as its first president. The seventy-four-year-old Donald Douglas Sr stayed on as honorary chairman of the board. His son, forty-seven-year-old Donald Douglas Jr, who had taken over as president of Douglas in 1956, was replaced in 1968 by Jackson McGowan, the former head of the Douglas Aircraft Division at Long Beach. Douglas Jr remained with the new company until 1973.

On 19 February 1968 an order from American Airlines for twenty-five DC-10s plus an option for a further twenty-five led to the development of the DC-10 tri-jet airliner programme. A month later the project was almost stillborn when Lockheed announced that orders for 144 L-1011 TriStars had been received from five major airlines. However, on 25 April 1968 United Air Lines placed a record order for thirty DC-10s with thirty more on option. In October Northwest Orient Airlines placed an order for the first DC-10-30 intercontinental model of the aircraft and the KSSU group followed suit in June 1969. Unfortunately, a downturn in airline business and bad publicity as a result of two major accidents meant that the DC-10's potential was never fully realised, although in 1977 the

Go tell it to the Marines! Three of McDonnell Douglas' famous jets for the USMC, the A-4M, the F-4J and the AV-8A, fly in formation. Douglas turned out 2,960 A-4 Skyhawks, while the McDonnell Company built a total of 5,068 Phantoms.

Air Force ordered the first of sixty KC-10 Advanced Tanker/Cargo versions. Production was terminated at the start of 1989 after 446 aircraft had been completed.

Fortunately for McDonnell Douglas, the Super 80 version of the DC-9, which was given the go-ahead on 19 October 1977, was ultimately to prove very successful and attractive short-term lease deals with airlines enabled the company to keep its Long Beach DC-9 production lines open. Despite cutbacks following the withdrawal from Vietnam, McDonnell's undoubted pedigree in the field of US fighter aircraft was further enhanced in 1973 with the selection of the F-15 Eagle as the USAF's next-generation, air-superiority and ground-attack fighter to replace the McDonnell-built F-4 Phantom. On 9 November 1978 McDonnell Douglas entered a new era with the first flight of the YAV-8B vertical take-off aircraft, part of a co-operative effort with British Aerospace and the on-going 'super' Harrier programme for the USAF and RAF.

The year 1979 marked the end of an era for two other famous McDonnell and Douglas aircraft designs. On 27 February 1979 the 2,960th and final Douglas A-4 Skyhawk was delivered and on 25 October the 5,068th and last McDonnell-built F-4 Phantom was received by the USAF. McDonnell Douglas, meanwhile, had received a contract to develop the F/A-18C Hornet as a replacement multi-mission aircraft to supersede not only the F-4 and A-4 but also the Vought A-7E attack aircraft in USMC and USN service. The F/A-18 (MD Model 267) had originated as a result of a congressional decision on 28 August 1974, which had instructed the USN to select one of the Air Force-sponsored lightweight fighter projects, the General Dynamics YF-16 or the Northrop YF-17, as the NACF (Navy Air Combat Fighter). An enlarged and much improved version of the YF-17, developed jointly by McDonnell Douglas and Northrop, was declared the winner of the NACF competition on 2 May 1975 and a contract was placed in November for nine

On 28 April 1967 the McDonnell Douglas Company came into existence and in February 1968 interest from American Airlines led to the development of the DC-10 tri-jet airliner programme. The DC-10 remained in production for over twenty years, during which 446 aircraft were built.

single-seat and two two-seat full-scale development aircraft. The F/A-18C was flown for the first time on 3 September 1987 and the first F/A-18C was delivered to the USN on 23 September 1987.

The beginning of the 1980s was marked by the deaths of James S. McDonnell on 22 August 1980 and Donald Douglas on 1 February 1981. Gloomy predictions of a downturn in commercial airline sales caused by a world-wide recession and stiff competition among manufacturers was not helped by news of the cancellation, in January 1982, of the contract for the C-X (C-17) advanced cargo aircraft which McDonnell Douglas had won in August 1981. The military sector, however, was generally quite buoyant and, late in 1981, a joint Douglas Aircraft-British Aerospace-Sperry team led by McDonnell Douglas resulted in the T-45 variant of the BAe Hawk 60 being selected as the winner of the Navy VTXTS training aircraft competition. On 27 August 1985 the McDonnell Douglas Helicopter Company (MDHC) was created with the purchase of the Hughes Helicopter Company. One of the designs acquired in the move was the AH-64 which was put into full-scale production in a new plant at Falcon Field, Mesa, Arizona, as the Apache for the US Army. The civil variant became the MD 500 and 530 series of light helicopters.

Although the Air Force had not proceeded with full-scale development of the C-X (C-17) advanced cargo aircraft first time around, it finally awarded a full-scale development contract to McDonnell Douglas for one flying prototype and two structural-test aircraft on 31 December 1985. The C-17A made its first flight on 15 September 1991 and, to date, 120 C-17A Globemaster IIIs have been approved to the year 2004.

In 1998 the C-17A was one of four McDonnell Douglas military models then in production – the F-15 Eagle, F/A Hornet, and T-45 being the other three – when the corporation was acquired by the Boeing Company, one of Douglas's earliest rivals.

One

Cavalry in the Clouds

The Davis-Douglas Company Cloudster was built in 1921 in an attempt to make the first non-stop flight across the US from coast to coast. On 27 June 1921 the Cloudster took off for New York, but the flight ended abruptly when engine failure forced it down at Fort Bliss, near El Paso, Texas.

Posing beside the wooden hull of the Cloudster at Wiltshire Boulevard in 1921 are, from left to right, Bill Henry, a Los Angeles Times writer, Eric Springer, the Douglas test pilot who made the first flight in the Clousdter on 24 February, a USN officer, David Davis, Donald Douglas and Jim Goodyear.

The DT, the military version of the Cloudster for torpedo-bombing, was the first Douglas aircraft built in quantity. DT-1A6031, pictured, was built in the Goodyear airship hangar in East Los Angeles and first flew early in November 1921. Douglas built forty DT-2 float-plane/land-planes for the US Navy, one DT-2B for Norway, and four DTBs for Peru. Another forty-four DTs were built by licensees.

In August 1923 the Army Air Service ordered five DT-2s from the Navy production run as Douglas World Cruisers, with interchangeable wheel and float landing gears, for the first round-the-world flight. On 17 March 1924 four of the DWCs left Clover Field at Santa Monica and headed for Alaska. Two of the DWCs were lost but *Chicago* (pictured), flown by Capt. Lowell H. Smith and Lt Leslie P. Arnold, and *New Orleans*, piloted by Lts Erick H. Nelson and John Harding, successfully completed the 27,534 mile journey in 175 days, arriving at Seattle on 28 September. The journey involved fifteen days, eleven hours and seven minutes of actual flying time.

New Orleans, pictured being refuelled, was the other DWC to reach Seattle in the historic flight.

As a result of the success of the round-the-world flight and encouraged by the Navy's procurement and manufacture of DT-2 torpedo-bombers, the US Army Air Service/Air Corps began ordering derivatives of the Cloudster as O-2 Corps Observation aircraft (O-2B pictured) in 1924. Between 1924 and 1936 Douglas delivered no less than 885 of these observation biplanes in more than fifty versions, including 108 for Mexico, China and Peru. Included in this grand total are 770 machines for the US Services – the Army (including 246 ordered for the Army Air Service/Air Corps), the National Guard, the Marine Corps and the Coast Guard.

In 1925 the Army Air Service ordered twenty-seven six/seven-passenger transport versions of the Douglas World Cruiser under the designation C-1, its first ever designated transport aircraft. The C-1 was designed to be able to carry a second Liberty engine as freight.

Douglas built fifty-nine M-series mail planes between 1925 and 1926, including fifty M-3s and M-4s (M-4 NX1475 pictured) for the US Post Office Department. These were almost identical to the Liberty-engined O-2s but had all military equipment deleted and a completely different cockpit layout.

The PD-1 was Douglas' first patrol bomber built for the US Navy and first flew in May 1929. In total, twenty-five PD-1s were built. These were followed by twelve T2D-1 (Second Douglas Torpedo – First Version) aircraft and, from 1930, by a second batch of eighteen, now re-designated P2D-1 (Patrol).

In 1929 Douglas began building commercial amphibians and pinned great hopes in the Sinbad prototype, but the Wall Street Crash and subsequent depression saw only eleven of the fifty-eight Dolphin production models being sold. The unsold Dolphins were bought by the Navy (which purchased nine RD-2s and -3s), the Coast Guard (which picked up fourteen, including the Sinbad prototype and the RD Dolphin pictured) and the Army Air Corps (which took delivery of twenty-four Dolphin Is and IIIs). The other Dolphin was bought by the Argentine navy.

The all-metal YO-31/Y10-43, O-43A, O-46A series of Douglas Observation Monoplanes of the early to mid-1930s were not as numerous as the biplane series had been a decade earlier. Nonetheless, 124 were produced for the US Army Air Corps (pictured is a US Army O-46A with enclosed cockpit) and three for the National Guard.

Meanwhile, in February 1929 the Army Air Corps directed that Douglas and Fokker, respectively, modify the experimental XO-35 and XO-27 monoplane observation aircraft that were on order to light bomber configuration. In 1930 Douglas delivered the gull-winged XO-35 observation and XB-7 bomber prototypes and consequently received orders for seven Y1B-7s (as pictured, with its four-man crew) and five Y10-35s.

TBD-1s in formation in January 1941. Designed in 1934, the Devastator was the first all-metal, monoplane carrier aircraft when it joined the fleet in 1937. It was also the first operational American naval aircraft to feature hydraulically operated folding wings. By modern standards it was too slow, with a poor rate of climb and a limited range. The Mk13 torpedo, whose pre-war development had suffered badly because of the lack of funding and limited testing, was very unreliable. It required that runs be made at 80ft altitudes at no more than 80 knots (92mph) with release no further than 1,000 yards from the target. Even so, the torpedo often failed to work properly. When America went to war in the Pacific in 1942 only about 100 TBD-1s were available and just twenty-five took part in the Battle of the Coral Sea on 7-8 May 1942.

The B-18 Bolo was derived from the DC-2 transport. A contract for 133 Bolos was issued in January 1936, after the prototype DB-1 (Douglas Bomber 1) won an August 1935 USAAC competition to find a replacement for the Martin B-10. A further 177 Bolos were ordered in June 1937. The type was finally replaced in service by the B-17 in 1942.

The B-23 Dragon, pictured here on 29 August 1940 over Mt Rainier, was an improved B-18 with a redesigned fuselage and, for the first time in an American bomber, a tail-gun position. Thirty-eight B-23s were ordered and the first flew on 27 July 1939. Most were used for a brief interlude on Pacific coastal patrol before being relegated to training and transport roles.

The XBLR-2, photographed as it neared completion at Santa Monica, was re-designated the XB-19 (38-471) and, as such, flew for the first time on 27 June 1941.

The second SBD-1 (Bu.No.1597) assigned to the Commanding Officer of VMB-2 at San Diego, the first unit to take delivery of the Dauntless, was one of fifty-seven SBD-1s built for the USMC in 1940.

SBD-3 production at El Segundo, with airframes 1151-1159 and beyond under assembly. Altogether, 858 SBD-3s were built, the first being delivered on 18 March 1941. Dauntlesses distinguished themselves in the Battle of the Coral Sea in May 1942 and at Midway in June, sinking the Japanese aircraft carriers *Akagi*, *Kaga*, *Soryu* and *Hiryu*, for the loss of 40 out of 128 attacking aircraft.

An SBD-3A (A-24A), one of seventy-eight with the deck hook removed, delivered from the US Navy production line at El Segundo between June and October 1941 with 'US Army' stencilled on the tail. In November 1941 fifty-two A-24As were shipped to the Philippines for use by the 27th Bomb Group (Light) but subsequent operational use in the Dutch East Indies and from Australia revealed that they lacked range, were too slow and were vulnerable to enemy fighters. In total, 763 A-24As (SBD-4 equivalent) and A-24Bs (SBD-5 equivalent) were built.

SBD-5s in flight. This was the main Dauntless production version. The first of 2,964 aircraft reached the USN in February 1943 and no less than twenty USMC squadrons were equipped with the SBD until late 1944.

Originally designed in 1938 as an attack bomber, the A-20 ranks among the most famous of its type during the Second World War. Its design was actually begun in 1936 by Jack Northrop before his company was acquired by the Douglas Corporation. Ed Heinemann's design team improved the breed, adding the first tricycle nose-wheeled gear on an American military aircraft and more powerful TwinWasps. The Model 7B, as it was re-designated, was entered for the July 1938 attack-bomber design competition and the prototype (pictured) flew on 26 October 1938.

On 15 February 1939 France ordered 100 DB-7 production aircraft, the first of which flew on 17 August that year. Sixty-four aircraft reached the Armèe de l'Air, entering combat on 31 May 1940 and seeing limited action before the French surrender. On 25 June Britain took over all French contracts and undelivered aircraft, including a contract for 170 DB-7s ordered by France in October 1939. In RAF service all fifteen Boston Is were used as trainers while about 200 Boston IIs (DB-7 and DB-7As) were converted to Havoc Is for night-fighting and night-intruder operations.

Meanwhile, early in 1939 the US Army Air Force had ordered 143 A-20As, delivered to light bombardment groups in the USA and Hawaii. A simultaneous order for sixty-three A-20s which were to be fitted with R-2600-7 turbo-super-charged engines was not proceeded with and all except one (which became the XP-70 night-fighter prototype) were used as photo-reconnaissance aircraft. Pictured are two P-70 night-fighters equipped with airborne interception radar and ventral gun tray.

On 20 February 1940 Britain ordered the DB-7B version (Boston III, AL399 is pictured), similar to the A-20A but with .303 inch guns in place of the .30 calibre models as well as Wright R-2600-A5B Cyclones instead of the R-2600-3s. These first entered service with No. 88 Squadron at Swanton Morley, Norfolk, in October 1941, where they replaced the Blenheim IV.

On 2 October 1940 the AAF ordered 999 A-20B models, powered by Wright R-2600-11 engines and fitted with self-sealing fuel tanks, armour plate, increased fuel tankage and .50 calibre guns in place of all but one of the earlier .30 calibres. Deliveries to the AAF commenced in December 1941. With American entry into the war, 162 Douglas-built and 194 Boeing-built models for the RAF were diverted to the AAF where the type was universally known as the Havoc after the British version. These attack bombers had a solid 'gun nose' with awesome firepower supplied by 20mm cannon and .50 calibre machine guns.

With war on other fronts taking precedence, some 151 Bostons were relinquished by the RAF for shipment to Russia. The Soviet Air Force received a total of 3,125 by the end of the war. Late in 1942 American deliveries to Britain were resumed, with 202 A-20C models supplied under lend-lease. This aircraft, similar to the DB-7B, was fitted with the R-2600-23 Cyclone and seven .30 calibre machine guns. It was known in RAF service as the Boston IIIA. In November 1942 the Boston entered RAF service in North Africa (these Boston IIIs are from No.114 Squadron) and, altogether, about 980 Boston IIIs and IIIAs were delivered to the RAF. Additionally, over 250 Boston IVs and Vs were transferred to the RAF from the USAAF, where they were designated A-20G and A-20J Havocs.

In US service the 5th Air Force operated the A-20 at masthead-height in the Pacific and used the aircraft to excellent effect during the Battle for Dutch New Guinea (an A-20 of the 389th Bomb Squadron, 312th Bomb Group is pictured in New Guinea). The 47th Bomb Group of the 12th Air Force used A-20s in the Italian campaign.

On 16 April 1942, in 'Ramrod 20', twelve Bostons of No.226 Squadron No.2 Group attacked the power station at Le Havre, France. The second box of six bombed from 14,500ft, 500ft above the leading box. Direct hits were scored on the power station, interrupting the electricity supply for forty-eight hours and gutting 75ft of the northern end of the main building. All the Bostons returned safely, although eleven received flak damage.

33

The final operational RAF version of the Havoc was the three-seat intruder variant of the DB-7B Boston III, carrying a gun-pack under the fuselage. It operated with No.418 'City of Edmonton' Squadron RCAF from March 1942 and with No.605 Squadron from July to October 1942 (pictured is BD112 YP-T of No.418 Squadron RCAF).

Pilot Officer (P/O) Al Lukas's all-American crew beside their Boston III (A-20C Havoc) W8317 'V-Victoria'. Lukas scored No.418 'City of Edmonton' Squadron's first aerial victory, a Ju 88 night-fighter, on the night of 6 May 1942, when he dropped his bomb load of three 250lb impact bombs and ninety 4lb incendiaries over the runway at Gilze Rijen, Holland, as the Junkers prepared to land. Five other Ju 88s were damaged in the blasts. The navigator, Sgt Bill Randolph, left, came from Memphis while Lukas hailed from Chicago and Sgt Harry Haskell, gunner, right, came from Boston.

On 7 May 1942 six Bostons of No.226 Squadron No.2 Group, led by P/O W.J. O'Connell attacked the power station at Ostend from 11,000ft in 'Circus 164'. No.226 Squadron was bracketed by intense flak, the base of a shell lodging just behind the head of Sgt Parsons, pilot of one of the Bostons. Three gunners were also wounded and immediately after the bombing Sgt Goodman broke formation, out of control, and the WOp/AG, Sgt Burt, bailed out (he became a POW). The photo shows the Boston (AL750 MG-Z) immediately after Burt had bailed out. Goodman regained control and flew back to make a safe landing at RAF Swanton Morley. A report received later stated that twenty-two coffins were delivered to the Germans by the local undertaker, a bomb having hit a listening post.

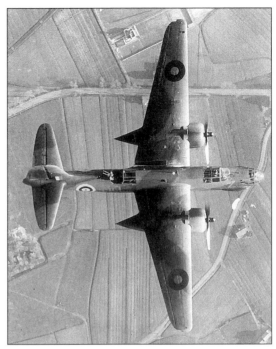

On 4 July 1942, Independence Day, six of the twelve A-20 Bostons of No.226 Squadron RAF at Swanton Morley, Norfolk, carried American crews of the 15th Bomb Squadron (Light) in attacks on four airfields in Holland. The senior-ranking US officer was Captain Charles Kegelman (second from left beside *Keg*), who attacked De Kooy airfield in AL750 'Z'. His starboard engine took a direct hit, burst into flames and the propeller flew off. The right wing tip struck the ground and the fuselage actually bounced on the surface of De Kooy aerodrome, tearing a hole in the belly of the bomber. Kegelman nursed the Boston safely home on one engine.

Sqdn Ldr J.C. 'Shaw' Kennedy DFC of No.226 Squadron climbs out of Boston Z2234 'H' upon his return from De Kooy airfield on 4 July 1942. Two American crews were lost.

No.2 Group's daylight 'tip and run' raids, designed to draw Luftwaffe fighters away from the Eastern Front, were often costly and the results disproportionate to the numbers lost. On 19 July 1942 twenty Bostons of Nos.88 and 226 Squadrons mounted raids in pairs on ten power stations in the Lille area, using low cloud as cover. One Boston nose-dived into the ground while making a bomb run on Mazingarbe power station and exploded in a wood east of Boulogne killing all three crew. A second Boston, flown by P/O Aubrey Niner of No.88 Squadron, was shot down while attacking the aerodrome at Lille-Nord and had to belly-land on a football pitch in Lille (pictured). The crew were captured.

Hits can be seen on the Finalens chemical works at Douvrin in this remarkable low-level photograph taken from Sgt Savage's Boston of No.88 Squadron during his attack of 22 September 1942.

Low level raiders. On 6 December 1942 No.2 Group mounted its most ambitious daylight raid so far – 'Operation Oyster' – sending eighty-four medium bombers, including thirty-six Bostons of Nos 88, 107 and 226 Squadrons, to bomb the Philips' Emmasingel valve and lamp factory and Stryp Group main works at Eindhoven, Holland. Pictured heading for the target are Bostons of No.88 Squadron, the nearest, AL749 'R-Robert', flown by P/O Jack Peppiatt of 'B' Flight.

A Boston turns away after bombing the Emmasingel valve and lamp factory on 6 December. The leading aircraft of No.88 Squadron attacked at rooftop-height with eleven-second-delay bombs and the remaining aircraft bombed at 1,000-1,500ft with HE and incendiary bombs. Fourteen aircraft – nine Venturas, one Mosquito, and four Bostons – failed to return.

In 1943 No.2 Group carried the war to the continent with 'Circus' raids (pictured is a No.88 Squadron Boston leaving the target at the Denain steel and armament works on 16 August 1943). Early in 1944 No.2 Group's bomber squadrons moved to southern England to carry the Second Tactical Air Force offensive to France in the build up to D-Day.

Air and ground crew of Boston III 'N-Nuts' *AVI RUMPERE AVISTIRCUS FACIRE* of No.88 Squadron at Hartford Bridge, late 1944.

Boston III 'B-Beer' *Beer Is Best* in No.88 Squadron. The Second Tactical Air Force moved to the continent in October-November 1944 to carry the war on to its conclusion. When production of this magnificent aircraft ended in September 1944, 7,098 Bostons had been built by Douglas and 380 by Boeing.

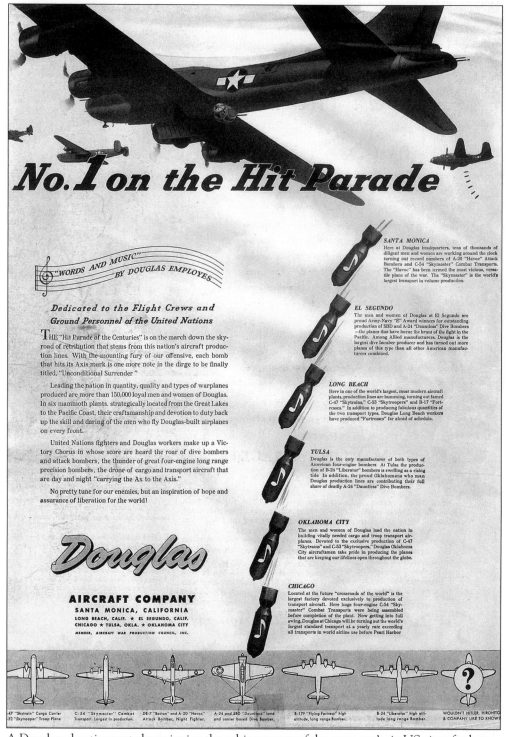

No.1 on the Hit Parade

"WORDS AND MUSIC" BY DOUGLAS EMPLOYES

Dedicated to the Flight Crews and Ground Personnel of the United Nations

THE "Hit Parade of the Centuries" is on the march down the sky-road of retribution that stems from this nation's aircraft production lines. With the mounting fury of our offensive, each bomb that hits its Axis mark is one more note in the dirge to be finally titled, "Unconditional Surrender"

Leading the nation in quantity, quality and types of warplanes produced are more than 150,000 loyal men and women of Douglas. In six mammoth plants, strategically located from the Great Lakes to the Pacific Coast, their craftsmanship and devotion to duty back up the skill and daring of the men who fly Douglas-built airplanes on every front.

United Nations fighters and Douglas workers make up a Victory Chorus in whose score are heard the roar of dive bombers and attack bombers, the thunder of great four-engine long range precision bombers, the drone of cargo and transport aircraft that are day and night "carrying the Ax to the Axis."

No pretty tune for our enemies, but an inspiration of hope and assurance of liberation for the world!

Douglas

AIRCRAFT COMPANY
SANTA MONICA, CALIFORNIA

LONG BEACH, CALIF. ★ EL SEGUNDO, CALIF.
CHICAGO ★ TULSA, OKLA. ★ OKLAHOMA CITY

MEMBER, AIRCRAFT WAR PRODUCTION COUNCIL, INC.

SANTA MONICA
Here at Douglas headquarters, tens of thousands of diligent men and women are working around the clock turning out record numbers of A-20 "Havoc" Attack Bombers and C-54 "Skymaster" Combat Transports. The "Havoc" has been termed the most vicious, versatile plane of the war. The "Skymaster" is the world's largest transport in volume production.

EL SEGUNDO
The men and women of Douglas at El Segundo are proud Army-Navy "E" Award winners for outstanding production of SBD and A-24 "Dauntless" Dive Bombers —the planes that have borne the brunt of the fight in the Pacific. Among Allied manufacturers, Douglas is the largest dive bomber producer and has turned out more planes of this type than all other American manufacturers combined.

LONG BEACH
Here in one of the world's largest, most modern aircraft plants, production lines are humming, turning out famed C-47 "Skytrains," C-53 "Skytroopers" and B-17 "Fortresses." In addition to producing fabulous quantities of the two transport types, Douglas Long Beach workers have produced "Fortresses" far ahead of schedule.

TULSA
Douglas is the only manufacturer of both types of American four-engine bombers. At Tulsa the production of B-24 "Liberator" bombers is swelling as a rising tide. In addition, the proud Oklahomans who man Douglas production lines are contributing their full share of deadly A-24 "Dauntless" Dive Bombers.

OKLAHOMA CITY
The men and women of Douglas lead the nation in building vitally needed cargo and troop transport airplanes. Devoted to the exclusive production of C-47 "Skytrains" and C-53 "Skytroopers," Douglas Oklahoma City aircraftsmen take pride in producing the planes that are keeping our lifelines open throughout the globe.

CHICAGO
Located at the future "crossroads of the world" is the largest factory devoted exclusively to production of transport aircraft. Here huge four-engine C-54 "Skymaster" Combat Transports were being assembled before completion of the plant. Now getting into full swing, Douglas at Chicago will be turning out the world's largest standard transport at a yearly rate exceeding all transports in world airline use before Pearl Harbor

C-47 "Skytrain" Cargo Carrier C-53 "Skytrooper" Troop Plane — C-54 "Skymaster" Combat Transport. Largest in production. — DB-7 "Boston" and A-20 "Havoc" Attack Bomber, Night Fighter. — A-24 and SBD "Dauntless" land and carrier based Dive Bomber. — B-17F "Flying Fortress" high altitude, long range Bomber. — B-24 "Liberator" high altitude, long range Bomber. — WOULDN'T HITLER, HIROHITO & COMPANY LIKE TO KNOW?

A Douglas advertisement championing the achievements of the company's six US aircraft plants.

40

A B-17F Flying Fortress on the Long Beach production line. Altogether, Douglas built 605 of the F models.

A third B-24 Liberator production line was brought into operation at the Tulsa, Oklahoma plant in March 1943.

All told, 962 B-24s, including 582 B-24Hs and 205 B-24Js, were turned out at the Tulsa plant during the Second World War.

B-17G-30-DL 42-38213 (olive drab) and B-17G-35-DL 42-106984 (natural metal finish) at the Douglas Long Beach factory. The latter did not leave the US, while the former was assigned to the 20th Bomb Squadron, 2nd BG, 15th AF and was lost on 7 July 1944 on the mission to Bleckhammer. Douglas-built G models were the first to become operational, the AAF receiving their first 'G' on 4 September 1943. Leaving the bomber unpainted speeded up production and increased overall flight performance. Douglas built 2,395 G models.

A Rosie's Riveter poses with B-17G-15-DL 42-37846, which together with 42-37876 (background) was delivered to Dover in September 1943. The former went on to fly in the 331st BS, 94th BG, 8th AF, while 42-37876, which was allocated to the 412th BS, 95th BG, and named *Miss-Raps-O-Dee*, was lost on 11 April 1944.

B-17G-75-DL 42-3543 *Sack Time Suzy*, in the 338th Bomb Squadron, 96th BG, 8th AF was one of sixty-eight B-17s interned after landing in neutral Sweden during the Second World War. Flight Officer (F/O) Rodney S. Greene and the crew landed at Bulltofta on 9 October 1943 and were interned. In 1945 the aircraft became one of seven converted to fourteen-seat airliners by Svenska Aeroplan AB (SAAB), who registered the aircraft as SE-BAH. It served ABA as *Sam* until being used for fire practice in September 1946.

B-17G-30-DL 42-38113 was the 1,000th Fortress built by Douglas at Long Beach, California. It was assigned to the 750th Bomb Squadron, 457th BG at Glatton, Cambridgeshire, and named *Rene III* in honour of the wife of the CO, Colonel James R. Luper. On 7 October 1944 *Rene III* was shot down on the mission to Politz. Seven crew members, including Luper, survived.

In post-war years PB-1Ws like XD1, Bu.No.77237 (B-17G-95-DL44-83874), were fitted with an AN/APS-20 sea-search radar and used by the USN on anti-submarine and weather reconnaissance duties. XD1 was retired in July 1956, put on the civil register as N5236V and finally disposed of at Love Field in 1963.

B-17F-75-DL 42-3521 served in the 8th AF and the AFSC before returning to the US in June 1944. In March 1945 it was transferred to the USN as PB-1 Bu.No.34106. The Philadelphia experimental station used it for various duties, including launching an instrumented scale model of an F8F-1 Bearcat under radio control to obtain high-speed data that could not be obtained in a wind tunnel.

A-26B-45-DL 44-34216. It was planned to replace all other medium aircraft with the A-26 Invader and on 10 July 1942 the XA-26 flew for the first time. Delivery of the A-26B began in August 1943. It proved to be the fastest American attack plane of the Second World War, with a top speed of 355mph, and packed no fewer than twenty-two guns. A-26Bs normally carried six nose-mounted guns, four blister guns on the fuselage sides and eight guns in four optional under-wing pods, as well as two top-turret and two belly guns.

Glass-nosed A-26C medium bombers, with a co-pilot/bombardier added as a fourth crew-member, replaced the A-20 in combat units and won the admiration of the crews who flew them. The A-26C had only six machine guns – two in the nose and two in each turret – and was capable of 370mph. The A-26C's speed, good range, bomb bay space and gloss-black paint (like A-26C *King of Diamonds*) made it ideal for low-level, spy-dropping 'Carpetbagger' missions over occupied Europe. During the moon period in 1945 they were used to drop twenty-eight teams of OSS agents deep into Germany.

The Invader flew its final mission in Europe on 3 May 1945, when 130 A-26s of the 9th AF, led by PFF Marauders, bombed the Stod Ammon Plant in Czechoslovakia. Only six A-26 groups were in service overseas by August 1945. In the Pacific they were operated by the 3rd BG in the 5th AF and the 319th BG in the 7th AF until 12 August 1945. However, the Invader, like this USN JD-1D, was used operationally in Korea. Some 142 A-26Cs were supplied to the Navy as JD-1 and JD-1D target-towing and drone-control planes (re-designated UB-26J and DB-26J in 1962).

The On Mark Engineering Company of Van Nuys built forty B-26Ks with completely rebuilt wings and fuselage, 2,500hp water-injection R-2800-103W engines, wing-tip tanks and electronics equipment. The YB-26K COIN (COunter-INsurgency), which first flew on 28 January 1963, carried 8,000lbs of assorted wing-mounted weapons plus a 4,000lb payload in the bomb bay and eight .50 calibre machine-guns in the nose. The B-26K first flew on 26 May 1964 and in June the first squadron was despatched to Thailand for night interdiction missions against the Ho Chi Minh Trail, the last sorties being flown on 9 November 1969.

In all, 2,452 Invaders were built. A-26C 43-22612 N3710G *Double Trouble* owned by Euroworld and operated by the Cavalier Air Force, was destroyed in a crash at the Biggin Hill Air Show on 21 September 1980, killing everyone on board.

A-26B 41-39427, which now flies as *Spirit of Waco* in the CAF, undergoing maintenance at Long Beach in 1987.

Opposite: Undoubtedly the most famous of all transports, the Douglas Commercial 3 (DC-3) was built in many versions and served in many guises, especially as a military transport in the Second World War, when it became universally known as the 'Gooney Bird' and as the Dakota. When production ended in the summer of 1945, some 10,926 had been built, including 10,123 as military transports under several USAAF designations, mainly C-47 and C-53. C-47A-1-DK 42-92099 *Iron Ass* was one of 2,299 C-47A-DKs built at Oklahoma City.

Two
Airliners and Transports

The single DC-1 (Douglas Commercial Type 1) X223Y on its first flight on 1 July 1933, three months after the rival Boeing Model 247 had entered airline service with United.

The DC-1, pictured at the Grand Central Air Terminal in Glendale, California, was designed in response to a requirement by TWA, which had first tried to purchase the Model 247. Boeing had an interest in United Airlines and could not deliver until all sixty 247s had been accepted by United. TWA could not wait and in August 1933 placed an initial order with Douglas for twenty of an improved DC-1 version called the DC-2.

The DC-2 (NC13711) first flew on 11 May 1934 and 198 examples were eventually produced in three commercial and eight military transport versions. In late August-early September, PH-AJU, the first DC-2-115 purchased by KLM, arrived at Rotterdam by ship from the USA, its wings dismantled. In 1984, for the DC-2's 50th anniversary, a DC-2 was painted in the representative colours of PH-AJU and flown from Schiphol Airport, Amsterdam.

In October 1934 KLM entered the airliner, now called *Uiver* (Stork), in the Melbourne Centenary Air Race between England and Australia. It was piloted by two Dutchmen, K.D. Parmentier and J.J. Moll, with two crew, Prins and Brugge, as navigator and flight mechanic respectively and carried four passengers and mail. Here, *Uiver* gets a helping hand from the people of Albary, Australia, 125 miles from the finish, after becoming bogged down. *Uiver* won the handicap prize, finishing second in the speed contest with an elapsed time of 90 hours, 17 minutes. It covered the distance at an average speed of 136.832mph.

In the late spring of 1934 interest shown by American Airlines in an aircraft larger than the DC-2 and designed for sleeper services led to the development of the DST (Douglas Sleeper Transport), first of the now-legendary DC-3 series. Construction of the first DST (X14988) began in December 1934 and it flew on 17 December 1935 at Clover Field, Los Angeles (pictured).

American Airlines' DC-3-144s and DC-3-277Ds, lined up at the company's Tulsa headquarters. The DC-3 (DST-144/NC16001) began scheduled operations on 25 June 1936. By December 1941, when the USA became embroiled in the Second World War, a total of forty DST/DST-As, 380 DC-3/3As (daytime transport versions) and ten DC-3Bs (combination sleeper/daytime transports built for TWA) had been delivered.

DC-2 PH-AKK of KLM. The one black spot of 1936 for KLM occurred on 9 December. Attempting to take off in fog, a DC-2 clipped the surround nets of tennis courts beside Plough Lane, demolished the cupola of a house on the north side of Hillcrest Avenue as it veered to the left, then cartwheeled over the road and crashed against the front of a house. Fourteen people on the aircraft were killed including the pilot, Captain Hautzmeyer.

The interior of a DC-2 executive transport.

KLM DC-2 *Pelikaan*.

KLM DC-3 PH-ALP in flight in the late 1930s. KLM was the first European airline to operate the DC-3. In May 1940, as the Nazis invaded Holland, courageous KLM crews attempted to bring their aircraft out of Schiphol. Three succeeded, flying two bullet-riddled DC-2s and a DC-3 to Croydon. Eighteen KLM aircraft were destroyed by the bombing of Schiphol. A further eleven were seized by the Germans. In all, fourteen were outside Holland, a total of seven finding their way to England.

The sumptuous interior of a KLM DC-3. On 10 August 1940 KLM started a service under charter to BOAC between Whitchurch aerodrome, Bristol, and Lisbon. This service continued throughout the war and was extended to Gibraltar in 1942. On 1 June 1943 a KLM DC-3 piloted by Captain Quirinus Tepas, flying from Portela airport, Lisbon, to Bristol, was shot down by Ju 88s in the Bay of Biscay. All four crew and the thirteen passengers were killed, including British film idol Leslie Howard, who had been lecturing on the stage and cinema in Spain and Portugal.

C-47-DL *Sad Sack* 41-1853(?). Named Skytrain by the USAAF, this was the first fully militarised version of the DST/DC-3 series. Beginning on 23 December 1941, 965 were delivered.

The XCG-17 was an experimental troop-transport glider created in the summer of 1944 at Clinton County Army Base in Ohio by removing the engines and fairing over the nacelles of C-47-DL41-18496. The aircraft was later re-engined and sold as surplus.

C-47A-45-DL 42-24119. Some 2,954 C-47A-DLs were produced at Long Beach while 2,299 C-47A-DKs were built at Oklahoma City, making the A version the most numerous of all the C-47 variants.

A USAAF C-47 in the North African desert.

A C-47 of the 439th TCG, 91st TCS, 9th Air Force about to snag the line to pull a Waco glider into the air. C-47s were used in every major allied airborne assault operation in 1944-1945, including the D-Day landings, Arnhem and the crossing of the Rhine. For his heroic sacrifice while flying a Dakota at Arnhem, Flt Lt David Lord of No.271 Squadron was awarded a posthumous VC.

Everywhere the fighters went the Dakota was sure to follow. This SEAC Dakota in India has a Spitfire for company. Dakotas joined No.31 Squadron on the Burma front in June 1942 and together with No.194 Squadron they flew supply missions for the Chindits in Burma.

XC-47C-DL 42-5671, fitted with Edo Model 78 single-step metal floats. Each float was fitted with two retractable wheels and provision was made for 300 US gallons (1,136 litres) of fuel. Edo were contracted for 150 sets of floats and C-47C amphibians were used on a limited basis in Alaska and New Guinea.

A C-47 being completed overhauled by engineers at BAD 2 (Base Air Depot), at Warton, near Liverpool, England, during the Second World War.

The same aircraft, now completed and renamed *Jackpot*.

RAF Dakotas at Kohima in 1945. At least one pilot was awarded the DFC for flying mules, thirty at a time, over the 'Hump' (the Himalayas) into Burma! In total, the RAF received 1,928 Dakotas during the Second World War.

After the war, surplus C-47s came into their own with emergent airlines around the globe while more than 200 pre-war civil DC-3s were still in operation with the airlines. Pictured is VT-ATT of Indian National Airways.

Thousands of surplus C-47s and C-53s were sold off by the US government and many, like C-47 SM-29, in Italian Air Force livery, found their way to foreign forces.

Ex-US C-47B-10-DK 43-49111, one of several operated by the Greek Air Force. In 1949, the Elliniki Vassiliki Aeroporia received thirty rebuilt C-47s with special USAF serial numbers. These were used as makeshift bombers during the Greek Civil War and as transports in the Korean War.

DC-3 PH-SSM of Airways Rotterdam.

A DC-3 of Air India.

C-47 GA+111 of the German Air Force.

Ex-USAF C-47A-85-DL 43-15613 of the Kongelige Norske Flyvapen (Royal Norwegian Air Force).

USN R4D-5L (LC-47H) Bu.No.12418, flown by Lt Cdr Conrad Shinn, taking off from the South Pole campsite for McMurdo Sound, Antarctica, on 21 November 1956. A total of eighty-one C-47A-DLs ordered by the USAAF, including 12418, were transferred to the US Navy. In addition, a further 157 C-47A-DKs were added to USN stocks.

R4D-5 Bu.No.12438 of the US Navy pictured at NAS Miramar. Many R4D-5s were modified for a variety of special duties including air-sea warfare training, navigation training, RCM and personnel transport.

Dakota IV KN434 of 1325 Flight RAF at Prestwick. During the Berlin Airlift of 1948-49, the Dakota equipped nine squadrons of RAF Transport Command. Some 105 USAF military DC-3s were used during the airlift, beginning on 26 June 1948.

RAF Dakota IV KN452 of No.21 Squadron was still based at Aden, together with KJ955, as late as the summer of 1966. The RAF's last Dakota was retired on 1 April 1970.

A C-47 Dakota of the Royal South African Air Force.

During the Vietnam War, Dakotas again proved their worth, not just as transports but also as electronic, psychological and reconnaissance aircraft (SC-47D, EC-47P, EC-47Q, and EC-47N).

Heavily armed 'Spooky' C-47 gun-ships, nicknamed 'Puff The Magic Dragon', served in South-east Asia in a night attack role. This AC-47D gun-ship served in the 4th SOS, 14th SOW in Vietnam.

The DC-4, later designated DC-4E (Experimental) was a brave attempt in 1936 to create a four-engined airliner capable of carrying forty-two passengers by day or thirty by night. Five airlines invested $100,000 each towards the project but the aircraft was too complex for its own good and PanAm and TWA later withdrew their support. The single DC-4E flew on 7 June 1938 and was subsequently sold to Japan, where it was lost in a crash in Tokyo Bay.

At the request of American, Eastern and United Air Lines, all further development was channelled into the less complex DC-4 project but America was to enter the Second World War before the new airliner could enter service. Needing suitable four-engined transport aircraft, the USAAC commandeered the DC-4A Santa Monica production line early in 1942 and the first thirty-four aircraft were designated C-54 Skymasters. No prototype was built, the first production aircraft flying on 14 February 1942. A second production line was subsequently opened in Chicago and eventually 1,315 Skymasters were built (C-54A-DO 42-107457 pictured).

Post-war, the large numbers of military surplus C-54s available were snapped up by operators world-wide (a Netherlands Government Air Transport C-54 is shown here), severely reducing the potentially lucrative DC-4 airliner market so that only seventy-four DC-4-1009s were built. This version had no cargo door and was used as a passenger transport with accommodation for a crew of five and forty-four passengers in daytime use or twenty-two passengers when used as a sleeper transport.

In 1948 the Soviets sealed off Berlin from the outside world and on 26 June the Berlin Airlift began when the USAF started making flights from Frankfurt and two other bases using C-47s and C-54 Skymasters. Some thirty-five C-54s were transferred from bases in Alaska, the Caribbean and the US to transport supplies to Berlin.

Within three weeks the airlift was well under way with fifty-four C-54 Skymasters and 105 C-47 Skytrains carrying the load of the US effort. At the peak of operations, 204 C-54s and twenty-two R5Ds (the USN version of the C-54D) were in operation into and out of Berlin (Tempelhof in the US zone, and Gatow in the British zone). The airlift continued until the end of September 1949.

Quantas DC-4 VH-EBM, one of eight Skymasters used by the Australian airline, which first introduced the DC-4 into company service in 1949.

Some 1,163 Skymasters were operated by the USAF, some serving in the Korean Conflict between 1950 and 1953. Small numbers were still in use during the Vietnam War. Pictured is C-54E-15-DO 44-9133 at Itazuke AFB, Japan, at the time of the Korean War.

R5D-3 (C-54Q) Bu.No.56501, one of eighty-six C-54Ds transferred from the USAF to the USN. Most surviving R5D-3s were re-designated C-54Qs in 1962.

R5D-3Z (VC-54Q) Bu.No.56506, a USN staff transport variant belonging to VR-24.

The first DC-5 flew on 20 February 1939 but the anticipated large airline orders never materialised after problems with excessive tail buffet were revealed during its flight-test programme. Only twelve DC-5s were built.

C-74 Globemaster I 42-65410 on a test flight. This was before the separate cockpits side by side (which led to the C-74 being dubbed 'Old Bug Eyes' by many pilots) were replaced by a single canopy. Fourteen Globemaster Is were built in total.

C-124A-DL Globemaster II 51-0177 of MATS (Military Air Transport Service).

C-124C 52-958. The C-124C differed externally from the C-124A in having 3,800hp Pratt & Whitney R-1460-63A engines and the APS-42 Weather Search Radar in a nose radome. Some 243 C models were produced at Long Beach, taking the final total of Globemaster IIs built to 448.

The C-133A-DL Cargomaster was the first USAF transport specified for propeller-turbine power (T34-P-7Ws) and first flew on 23 April 1956. Fifty Cargomasters were built, late production models fitted with a clamshell-type rear loading door to accommodate Atlas ICBMs or Thor and Jupiter IRBMs.

C-133A-15-DL Cargomaster 56-2000 of MATS. The C-133As and Bs were taken out of MAC (Military Airlift Command) service in 1971following fatigue problems.

The DC-6 entered fleet operation with both American and United Air Lines on 27 April 1947. Despite early problems, the DC-6 proved very successful and some 704 DC-6, -6A and -6B (HB-IBO of Swissair at Kloten, Zurich, pictured) versions were built.

DC-6B YU-AFF of Adria Airways. The DC-6 continued to serve smaller airlines until well into the 1980s.

A DC-6 of the Italian Air Force. The USAF also acquired 101 C-118A military versions of the DC-6A for use by MATS Atlantic and Pacific divisions.

DC-6 HB-ILU of Balair.

A DC-6A of Air Ferry.

Many surplus DC-6Bs have been modified as aerial tankers, with the installation of a large external fuselage tank holding 2,500-3,000 US gallons of retardant, for fighting forest fires in the USA, South America and Europe. This DC-6 belonging to the Securité Civil was pictured in France in 1989.

The DC-7 was a direct development of the DC-6B with the fuselage stretched by 40in to add one row of seats. All 105 examples built were operated by US trunk carriers, the first beginning service with American Airlines on 4 November 1953. The DC-7 was followed by 112 DC-7Bs, and 121 DC-7Cs (Seven Seas), bringing the total production to 338 aircraft. The 7C had a span 10ft longer than previous models so it could carry more fuel and was the world's first commercial transport able to fly non-stop across the Atlantic in both directions (the DC-7B could not fly non-stop westbound against average winds). The DC-7C entered scheduled service with Pan Am on 18 April 1956. Pictured is DC-7C G-AOIA of BOAC, one of ten bought by the British airline.

DC-8-32 PH-DCD of KLM. The DC-8, which first flew on 30 May 1958, was a belated attempt to catch up with the Boeing 707, America's first commercial jet, but arrived too late to mount a serious challenge to Boeing.

DC-8-33 PP-PEA, the second built, of Varig. This aircraft was written off on 4 March 1967 at Monrovia, Liberia. In all, fifty-seven Series 30 aircraft were built.

KLM DC-8-32 PH-DCA *Albert Plesman*, named in honour of the airline's founder, who first helped satisfy Dutch public interest in flying immediately after the First World War when he organised an air transport exhibition in Amsterdam. The overwhelming success of the event encouraged Plesman to pursue his plan to form a Dutch air transport company, which grew into the famous airline KLM.

DC-8-32 PH-DCF of KLM, leased to Garuda Indonesian Airways. This aircraft was last operated as a cargo plane with Zantop International before being broken up in July 1978 at Detroit-Willow Run.

DC-8-30s and -50s of KLM at Schiphol. The DC-8 Series 50, which first flew on 20 December 1960, was the first DC-8 to be powered by turbo fan engines instead of turbo jets, and entered service with KLM on 3 April 1961.

DC-8-41 CF-TJA of Trans-Canada Airlines. A total of thirty-two Series 40s, all powered by Rolls-Royce Conway turbo fans, were built for Alitalia, Canadian Pacific and Trans-Canada.

DC-8-53 *Albert Schweitzer* PH-DCN of KLM. Eighty-eight DC-8-50s were built.

DC-8 *Orville Wright* of VIASA Venezolana Internacional. When DC-8-63 production finished on 12 May 1972 some 556 DC-8 models had been built.

DC-8-52 ZK-NZE of Air New Zealand. Apart from the eighty-eight Series 50 aircraft built, six Series 10 and four Series 30 aircraft were brought up to Series 50 standard.

DC-9-32 N3318L of Delta Airlines. Delta ordered fifteen DC-9s in May 1962 but only fifty-eight had been sold in total by the time the airliner made its first flight on 25 February 1965. Despite this poor start, the DC-9 became the most successful of the Douglas Commercial aircraft with 976 sold to airlines and the US military.

The DC-9 Series 10 first flew on 25 February 1965 and made its first in-service airline flight for Delta Airlines on 8 December 1965. In all, 140 Series 10 DC-9s were built for US and overseas airlines, the last being delivered to Aeronaves de México on 27 November 1968. DC-9-15 XA-SOF of Aeroméxico is shown in 1968.

DC-9-31 N903H of Hawaiian in 1968. Altogether, 621 Series 30s were built.

DC-9-32 YU-AJM of JAT.

DC-9-32 CF-TMD of Air Canada at Toronto in the late 1970s.

DC-9-32 HB-IFV of Swissair at Geneva on 9 September 1981. This aircraft is now operated by Northwest Airlines.

DC-9-32 N950PB, owned by Playboy. The last Series 30s were delivered to US Air in April 1982.

All three services of the US military operate the DC-9. In USAF service, twenty-three C-9A Nightingale aero-medical evacuation aircraft (derivative of the DC-9 Series 20 airliner) can each carry forty patients plus five medical staff. Pictured is C-9A 68-8932 of the 375th Aeromedical Airlift Wing of MAC in the US.

In Navy service, C-9B transports are operated by eight USN squadrons (Bu.No.159116 of VR-57 is pictured over the *Queen Mary*, berthed at Long Beach, California). C-9B transports are operated by the Marines from MCAS Cherry Point, North Carolina.

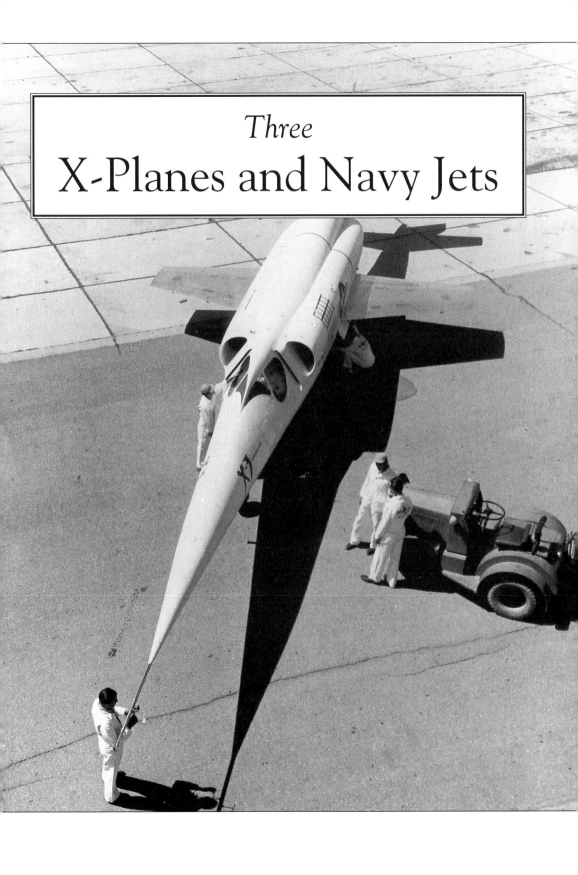

American high-speed fighters and bombers of the 1950s owed their initial development in no small measure to the German and British genius for aircraft and engine design. Captured German data on swept-wing and tailless aircraft, as well as jet and rocket development, was made available to American aircraft companies after the war. The influence it had on the development of American fighter and bomber aircraft was decisive. XB-43 *Mixmaster* 44-61508 (pictured), the first American jet bomber design, first flew on 17 May 1946 but did not enter production. It had a maximum speed of 507mph and a crew of three.

Three war-time Douglas designs which did not enter full-scale production were the two-seat XSB2D-1 bomber, intended as a replacement for both the Dauntless and the Curtiss Helldiver, the single-seat BTD Destroyer and the 3/4-seat XTB2D-1 Skypirate, first considered in 1942 as a single-engine, long-range torpedo-bomber for the new *Midway*-class USN carriers. Only two XTB2D-1s were built, powered by a Pratt & Whitney 28-cylinder, air-cooled, radial-driving, contra-rotating, four-blade propeller as pictured.

Previous page: The single X-3 Stiletto, 49-2892, which first flew on 20 October 1952, was built to investigate the design features of an aircraft suitable for sustained supersonic speeds. A secondary purpose of the aircraft was to test new materials such as titanium. Particular attention was given to the problem of 'pitch up', a phenomenon often encountered with swept-wing-configured aircraft.

America first captured the world's air speed record on 19 June 1947 when the Lockheed XP-80R Shooting Star, piloted by Col. Albert Boyd, reached 623.74mph at Muroc (later Edwards AFB), California. On 20 August Cdr Turner F. Caldwell, USN, eclipsed this record, achieving a speed of 640.7mph in the first D-558-1 Skystreak.

Five days after Caldwell's record-setting flight, on 24 August, Major Marion E. Carl, USMC, used the same D-558-I to increase the world absolute record to 650.92 mph.

D-558-1 Skystreak pictured on 10 September 1947.

Cdr Caldwell poses in front of the Douglas D-558-II Skyrocket. The USN project received a setback in May 1948 when the engine in one D-558-I exploded on take-off, killing the NACA test pilot Howard Lilly. The second D-558-I was stored to provide spare parts for the other and three new models, called 'Phase Two' aircraft, with swept wings, were built.

D-558-2 Skyrocket. In November 1953 Scott Crossfield became the first man to fly faster than twice the speed of sound after his D-558-II Skyrocket had been released from a B-29.

The X-3 Stiletto was powered by two Westinghouse J-34-WE-17 turbo-jets and was capable of take-off and landing under its own power. It possessed a top speed of just over Mach 1 and reached an altitude of 41,318ft. Failure of the J46 engine development programme was responsible for the X-3's inability to reach its Mach 2 design objective. 49-2892 is now displayed at the Air Force Museum in Dayton, Ohio.

In September 1953 the Hawker Hunter 3 re-captured the air speed record for Britain and the Supermarine Swift 4 then increased it to 735.70mph. America looked to Douglas and Ed Heinemann (right, with Cdr Turner F. Caldwell) to supply a record-breaking aircraft. On 14 September the XF4D-1 Skyray, fitted with the 11,600lb-thrust XJ40-WE-8B after-burner engine was put forward.

On 3 October 1953, 35-year-old war veteran Lt Cmdr James B. Verdin, USN, took off in the XF4D-I prototype from El Centro Naval Base, some forty miles from the Mojave Desert, and headed for the Salton Sea 3-km (1.86-mile) course. Verdin made four passes and set a new world speed record with an average speed of 752.94mph which stood until 28 August 1961 when it was beaten by the F4H Phantom.

The XF4D-I Skyray in which Lt Cmdr Verdin, USN, set the new speed record in October 1953.

Lt Cdr Verdin in the record-breaking Skyray.

On 16 October 1953 Douglas test pilot Robert O. Rahn set a new air speed record over a 100-kilometre (62.1-mile) course with an average speed of 728.11mph.

Major Edward N. LeFaivre, USMC, taking off from Point Mugu, California, on 22 May 1958 in a 3,000-metre climb.

On 26 May 1958, at Point Mugu, LeFaivre set five official aircraft climb records. The highest goal of 15,000 metres (49,212.5 feet) was reached in 2min, 36.05sec.

The Skyraider was conceived in the Second World War as the XBT2D-1 and became the AAD-1 when, on 11 March 1946, the Navy replaced the VB (dive) and VT (torpedo) designations for its bombers with 'VA' for 'attack' aircraft. Deliveries began in November 1946 of the first of 242 AD-1s and thirty-five AD-1Q radar-countermeasures versions. These were powered by the R-3350-24W. In December, the AD-1 entered service with VA-19A. Two years later, some eight carrier attack squadrons were equipped with the Skyraider.

AD-1 Skyraiders and F4U Corsairs from CVS-36 on the flight deck of the USS *Antietam* on 15 October 1951. When communist North Korea poured across the 38th Parallel on 25 June 1950, AD Skyraiders, or 'Able Dog' as the AD-1 was known, equipped twelve Navy squadrons, AD-4Ns equipped two night-attack squadrons and AD-3Ws equipped two early-warning squadrons.

The first USMC Skyraider squadron, VMA-121, arrived in Korea with AD-3s in October 1951 and began operations from land bases. Another seven Marine Corps Skyraider units would follow by the end of the war. During the war twenty-four Navy Skyraider squadrons were operational. Here, armourers attend to one of VA-115's AD-4Bs in Air Wing 11 aboard the *Philippine Sea* (CVG-11) in 1951.

Ex-USN Skyraider AEW I (AD-4W) WT121 of No.849 Squadron RNAS Culdrose, one of forty-five AEW Skyraiders supplied to the Royal Navy under the Mutual Defence Assistance Programme, deliveries of which began in November 1951.

A USN hunter-killer team composed of an AD-5 hunter (leading) and an AD-6 killer. When the Korean War ended there were twenty-four Navy Skyraider squadrons. By September 1955 this had risen to twenty-nine, and three versions of the AD-5 were in production as well as the AD-6 ground-support, single-seat aircraft. All told, no less than twenty-two versions of the Skyraider were built.

Four AD-6s from VA-75 on board the USS *Independence* (CVA-62) in 1960. Among the first carrier-borne aircraft in action in South-east Asia were A-1H/J (AD-6) Skyraiders, which flew the first retaliatory strikes against North Vietnam in August 1964. The 'Spad', as it was now known in the Navy, still had much to offer (two even shot down MiG 17 jets during the conflict) and a dozen squadrons were still in service aboard the fast-attack carriers, the same number as at the start of the Korean War. By 1968, A-6A medium-attack squadrons had replaced all A-1 Skyraiders on carriers.

Both the USAF and the South Vietnamese Air Force operated the single-seat A-1H and A-1J and two-seat A-1E and A-1G in Vietnam. USAF Skyraiders, popularly known as 'Dumptrucks', were ideal for close-support and interdiction missions along the Ho Chi Minh Trail, but their most famous Air Force role was as 'Sandy' escorts to rescue-helicopters, a service USAF Skyraiders provided until late in 1972.

The Model 1015 Cloudmaster II proved a vain attempt to capture an anticipated post-war boom in light aircraft sales. The prototype (s/n 43113, NX8000H) first flew on 12 March 1947 powered by two Continental E-250 engines driving a two-blade pusher propeller via a three-section drive-shaft. This arrangement proved unsatisfactory and the aircraft did not enter production.

The F3D (F-10) Skynight was the world's first carrier-borne jet night-fighter and flew on 23 March 1948. In Korea it was responsible for destroying more enemy aircraft than any other USN or USMC aircraft and was the first jet aircraft to destroy another at night when an F3D-2 from VMF (N)-513 (pictured) downed a Yak-15 on 2 November 1952.

Some 261 F3D aircraft were built and they served from 1950 until the Vietnam War. Pictured is F3D-2Q (EF-10B) Bu.No.127060 of VMCJ-3, USMC, one of thirty-five F3D-2s modified as ECM aircraft.

A2D-1 Skyshark, which flew on 26 May 1950. Two prototypes and ten production Skysharks were built but protracted power-plant and related gearbox problems and the emergence of the XA-4D-1 Skyhawk saw all further Skyshark development cancelled.

The delta-wing F4D-1 (F-6) Skyray, the 'Ten-minute killer' or 'Ford', as it was known, first flew on 23 January 1951, but its engine development was protracted and it was five years before the short-range interceptor entered squadron service, with VC-3, on 16 April 1956. Some 419 F4D-1 Skyrays (F-6A from 1962) were built (230 others were cancelled) and eleven first-line USN squadrons were equipped. The last Skyray was delivered to the USN on 22 December 1958.

The Skyray also equipped six operational USMC fighter squadrons (F4D-1 Bu.No.134804 of VMF-115, the first Marine squadron to be equipped, is shown in 1957) as well as three reserve squadrons and a number of specialized units. The last F4Ds were retired in 1964.

War in Korea in 1950 resulted in an urgent need for Boeing B-47 Stratojets and Douglas Tulsa was contracted to build ten B-47B-35-DTs and 252 B-47E Stratojets for Strategic Air Command.

On 31 March 1949 Douglas was awarded a two-prototype contract for the XA3D-1 two-jet bomber, which was the largest and heaviest aircraft capable of carrier operation. Ed Heinemann's design team's XA3D-1 first flew on 28 October 1952 with XJ40-WE-3 engines. Fitted with Pratt & Whitney J57-P-6 engines, A3D-1s were first delivered to the USN in December 1954. Pictured is Bu.No.135440, one of forty-nine first-production A3D-1s (A-3A) built. Note the radar-controlled tail turret.

The first 123 A3D-2 (A-3B) Skywarriors built (including Bu.No.138915, pictured) differed from the A3D-1 in having a strengthened airframe and were powered by the more powerful 10,500lb-thrust J57-P-10 engines. The next twenty were fitted with an air-refuelling probe. Altogether, 283 Skywarriors were built.

Thirty RA-3B (A3D-2P) photographic reconnaissance versions of the hugely successful Skywarrior series were built. The first A3D-2 flew on 22 July 1958. This A3D-2Q electronic reconnaissance variant shows the characteristic 'jowl' fairing which was installed on both sides of the forward fuselage and the circular camera porthole located above the fairing on each side of the aircraft.

Bu.No.142650 of VAQ-135 Det 1, one of thirty-nine EKA-3B combination ECM/tanker aircraft (thirty-four of which were modified from KA-3B tanker configuration by the Naval Air Rework Facility (NARF) at Alameda, in northern California). After 1975 most EKA-3Bs had their electronic equipment removed and were re-designated KA-3Bs.

A-4D-2 (A-4B) Skyhawk Bu.No.142700 of VA-216 refuels an EA-3B (A3D-2Q) Skywarrior of VQ-2 over the Mediterranean on 26 October 1967. Both squadrons were part of CVW-3 stationed aboard the attack aircraft carrier USS *Saratoga* (CVA-60) during her 1967 Mediterranean deployment. Some twenty-five A3D-2Q/RA-3B versions were built and they could be easily distinguished externally by the ventral 'canoe' fairing and square windows on the fuselage sides.

The A-4 (A4D) Skyhawk was conceived as a jet-powered successor to the AD-1 Skyraider in 1952, the XA4D-1 flying for the first time on 22 June 1954. Deliveries of A4D-1s to the USN began in September 1956. Here, an A-4 Skyhawk makes an arrested landing aboard the flight deck of the attack carrier USS *Coral Sea* (CVA-43) in March 1965.

The A-4 was among the first aircraft from Task Force 77 sent into action in South-east Asia. On 4 August 1964, sixty-four aircraft, including fifteen A-4Cs from CVW-14 aboard *Constellation* (CVA-64) and sixteen A-4Es from VA-55 'War Horses' and VA-56 'Champions' of CVW-5 aboard *Ticonderoga*, flew the first retaliatory strikes against North Vietnam, attacking communist naval vessels about seventy miles off the enemy coast. Vietnam was the target in September 1965 for these A-4Es (of VA-86 'Sidewinders' and VA-72 'Blue Hawks') and McDonnell F-4B Phantom IIs (of VF-41 'Black Aces') aboard *Independence* (CAV-62).

Affectionately known to its pilots as 'Scooter' because of the way it scooted like a balsa plane from the steam catapult, the A-4F, or 'Heinemann's Hot Rod' (after the Douglas chief engineer), became one of the most successful attack aircraft in fleet service between 1962 and 1975. The A-4F was also the mount of the USN's famous 'Blue Angels' Flight Demonstration Team, 1974-87, seen here in a Delta formation with NPTR El Centro in the background.

VMA-224 at MCAS El Toro, California, was the first USMC unit to be equipped with the Skyhawk, when it received its first A4D-1s in January 1957. The A4D-2 became operational in September, followed by the A4D-2N in March 1960 and the A-4E in December 1962. Pictured is a USMC TA-4F on a live-firing training mission. Two TA-4E advanced trainer prototypes were ordered in 1964 and 238 TA-4F production versions followed, deliveries beginning in May 1966.

TA-4F Bu.No.152850, showing the distinctive starboard-mounted air-refuelling probe. The majority of TA-4Fs built were later modified as TA-4Js, others becoming EA-4F 'electronic aggressors' and OA-4M tactical air co-ordinators for the USMC.

TA-4J Skyhawks of VT-25 in formation. Beginning in June 1969, 293 TA-4Js were operated by the US Naval Air Advanced Training Command.

Bu.No.157904 (NZ6201), the first of ten single-seat J52-P-8A-engined A-4Ks delivered in January 1970 to the Royal New Zealand Air Force. The RNZAF also acquired four two-seat TA-4Ks.

A-4Ks of 'Kiwi Red', the RNZAF Skyhawk formation aerobatic team.

Bu.No.158148, the first of 158 A-4Ms built for the USMC. The A-4M first flew on 10 April 1970 and many major improvements over previous models were introduced including the more powerful, 11,200lb-thrust J52-P-408A engine.

A-4M Bu.No.159471 of the USMC showing the distinctive humped avionics compartment first retrofitted to A-4E Skyraiders. The A-4M was the last version used by the US. Total A-4 production reaching 2,960, including overseas deliveries of new and surplus Skyhawks to the air forces of Argentina (A-4P), Singapore (A-4S), Israel (A-4H/N), Kuwait (A-4KU), Malaysia (A-4PTM), Australia (A-4G) and New Zealand.

RB-66C-DT Destroyers in December 1959. The B-66 was originally seen as an updated development of the A3D Skywarrior for the tactical light bomber and reconnaissance role, to replace the B-26 Invader which had been found lacking in Korea, but it evolved as a powerful ECM aircraft. Production began at Long Beach and later Tulsa, the first RB-66A flying on 28 June 1954.

RB-66C-DT 54-450. The first of thirty-six of these seven-seat electronic reconnaissance and countermeasures aircraft flew on 29 October 1955. ECM equipment was carried in the wing-tip pods, in the nose and later in place of the tail turret. A pressurized compartment replaced the bomb/camera bay of the B/RB-66B.

In the mid-1960s, fifty-two RB-66Bs were modified to EB-66Es to supplement existing active radar jammers.

The WB-66D-DT 55-391 was the final production version (weather reconnaissance) of the Destroyer, thirty-six of which were built. This took the total Destroyer production to 294 aircraft.

Four
McDonnell Douglas

On 28 April 1967 the McDonnell Douglas Company came into existence and the following year, on 19 February 1968, an order from American Airlines for twenty-five DC-10s plus an option for a further twenty-five led to the development of the DC-10 tri-jet airliner programme. The DC-10 prototype first flew on 29 August 1970. Production ended at the beginning of 1989 after 446 aircraft had been completed. Air New Zealand purchased eight DC-10 Series 30s, two of which are pictured.

DC-10 Series 30 EC-CBO *Costa Del Sol*, one of eight DC-10-30s purchased by Iberia.

DC-10 Series 30CF OO-SLC, one of five purchased by Sabena Belgian World Airlines. Thirty DC-10-30CF passenger/cargo convertible aircraft have been built and all were delivered between April 1973 and September 1984.

On 19 December 1977 the USAF ordered 20 tanker-cargo derivatives of the DC-10-30CF, designated KC-10A Extender. The first KC-10A (s/n 48200) flew at Long Beach on 12 July 1980 and eventually sixty KC-10 Extenders were built for the USAF, the last being delivered in 1988. The last DC-10s for airline service (ten DC-10-40Ds for JAL) were delivered between April 1976 and March 1983, taking total DC-10 production to 446 aircraft.

A USAF requirement in the mid-1960s for a long-term air-superiority fighter to outperform and outclass any enemy aircraft gained even greater priority in 1967 with the arrival on the world stage of the Soviet-built MiG 23 and MiG 25. Finally, on 23 December 1969, after study submissions from eight competitors had been considered, McDonnell Douglas' proposal was declared the winner and the company received governmental go-ahead for its F-15 programme. Twenty FSD (Full-Scale Development) aircraft (eighteen F-15As and two two-seat TF-15As) were ordered, with the F-15A making its maiden flight on 27 July 1972. Pictured is F-15B (TF-15A) 71-0291.

The first unit to receive the F-15A in the USA was the 555th Tactical Fighter Training Squadron, 58th Tactical Fighter Training Wing at Luke AFB, Arizona, in November 1974.

In the USAFE (Europe) the F-15A first equipped the 36th TFW at Bitburg AB, West Germany (75-0057 in the 36th TFW, pictured) and the 32nd TFS at Camp New Amsterdam, Holland.

In all, 384 F-15As were built, including nineteen for Israel. These were followed by sixty-one two-seat F-15Bs (including two for Israel), 473 F-15Cs (differing from the F-15A in having increased fuel capacity, FAST packs on the fuselage sides and enhanced radar capability) and eighty-five two-seat F-15Ds. A total of 532 Eagles were in the USAF inventory in 1998. Pictured is F-15B 73-0109.

The first F-15E Strike Eagle flew on 11 December 1986 and 221 were authorized for the USAF between February 1986 and February 1997. In 1998, 202 Es were in the USAF inventory (F-15E of the 48th TFW is shown at RAF Lakenheath). They differ from previous Eagles mainly in having a strengthened structure, additional avionics and increased air-to-ground weapon load. So far, total F-15 production is 1,003 examples, including the above 221 Es.

In 1972 MAC issued a specification for a new AMST (Advanced Medium Short Take-Off and Landing Transport) to replace its fleet of C-130 Hercules. Facing stiff competition from Bell, Fairchild and Lockheed, McDonnell Douglas' YC-15 and Boeing's YC-14 proposals were accepted and both companies were awarded preliminary design contracts in November 1972. A contract for two prototypes was received by each of the two companies in January 1973. The JT8D-17-turbo fan-powered 70-1875, the first of the two YC-15 prototypes, is seen here.

The second YC-15 (70-1876), powered by 18,000lb-thrust JT8D-209 turbo fans, in tactical camouflage. Fly-off trials were conducted for the USAF in late summer 1977, but the Air Force decided that the C-130 Hercules was still the most cost-effective tactical transport and that neither the YC-15 nor the YC-14 would meet its most pressing airlift requirements. Funding for the AMST project was withdrawn.

The Harrier was the world's first operational fixed-wing VSTOL aircraft and flew in development form on 31 August 1966 (the first true production aircraft flew on 28 December 1967). McDonnell Douglas obtained licence rights for the Harrier but the 102 AV-8As (Harrier Mk50) and eight two-seat TAV-8As (Harrier Mk54) ordered for the USMC in 1969 were built in the UK. The Naval Air Rework Facility at MCAS Cherry Point, North Carolina, subsequently modernized forty-seven AV-8As (including Bu.No.158387 of VMA-513, pictured) by upgrading them to AV-8C configuration.

The AV-8B was an advanced version of the Harrier with more powerful Rolls-Royce Pegasus 11 vectored-thrust turbo fans, a larger wing area built primarily of lightweight carbon-epoxy materials and several other improvements. Two AV-8As (Bu.Nos158394/95) were modified as YAV-8B prototypes. Bu.No.158394, pictured here in September 1978, flew for the first time on 9 November 1978 at St Louis.

Starting in early 1985, McDonnell Douglas built 300 AV-8Bs and twenty-eight TAV-8B two-seat trainers for the USMC, plus twelve EAV-8B Matadors for the Spanish Navy. Ninety-six GR.5s for the RAF have been assembled by British Aerospace from MCAIR kits. Pictured is a Rolls-Royce Pegasus 11 21,500lb-vectored-thrust turbo fan and the first YAV-8B prototype.

The F/A Hornet was conceived as a multi-mission aircraft to supersede the F-4 Phantom fighter, A-4 Skyhawk and A-7E attack aircraft in USMC and USN squadrons. Pictured is the prototype (Bu.No.160775), which was rolled out at St Louis on 13 September 1978 and first flew on 18 November. Hornets first went to sea in February 1985 with VFA-25 'Fist of the Fleet' and VFA-113 'Stingers', part of CVW-14 aboard the *Constellation*(CV-64).

Two F/A-18A Hornets of VFA-86. Altogether, 380 F/A-18As were built for the USN and USMC.

McDonnell Douglas built forty-one F/A-18B (TF/A-18A) two-seat trainers with full combat capability.

The F/A-18C Hornet flew for the first time on 3 September 1987. This version has the capability to carry the advanced medium-range air-to-air missile (AMRAAM), the Maverick air-to-ground missile and the infrared-imaging self-protection jammer. The first F/A-18C was delivered to the USN on 23 September 1987. McDonnell Douglas rolled out the first improved F-18E/F on 18 September 1995, with a first flight in November. The USN plans to acquire 1,000 F-18E/Fs to replace early F/A-18A/Bs and Grumman F-14s. Initial operational capability is planned for 2004.

In 1986 the USN Flight Demonstration Squadron, the *Blue Angels*, replaced its A-4Fs and began training with F/A-18As for the 1987 season (pictured).

The first Series 80 (or Super 80), a stretched version of the DC-9 with re-fanned engines and updated avionics, was the 909th DC-9 off the production line and was first flown on 18 October 1979. At first, sales of the DC-9-80 were slow, but attractive short-term lease deals led to an upsurge in interest. The DC-9-82 (MD-82) was first flown on 8 January 1981. Starting in 1983, McDonnell Douglas began officially referring to the DC-9-80 as the MD-80. Pictured is MD-82 HB-IKK (now I-SMEL) of Alisardia (now Meridiana) at Bologna on 30 May 1985.

The long-range MD-83, with extra fuel carried in two 580-gallon tanks in the cargo compartment, first flew on 17 December 1984. D-AGWB of German Wings is shown at Paris-Orly on 12 June 1989 (the aircraft is now operated by Aero Lloyd). By 1989, sales of the MD-80 series exceeded the DC-9 production total and the MD-80 went on to become the most successful airliner ever built at Long Beach.

An MD-83 of Oasis taking off from Palma in 1988.

MD-83 G-PATA of Paramount at Bristol on 16 August 1987. This aircraft is now operated by Spanair.

The MD-87 first flew on 4 December 1986. Pictured is OE-LMO of Austrian Airlines at Frankfurt in June 1994.

The MD-88 first flew on 15 August 1987. Pictured is EC-FLK of Aviaco at Paris-Orly on 1 June 1994.

The MD-80 prototype was modified as a demonstrator for ultra-high-bypass (UHB) prop-fan engines developed by General Electric and Allison and is seen here at Farnborough on 11 September 1988 with a port-mounted GE36 unducted fan engine. The P&W-Allison 578-DX prop-fan was also tried but by 1989 interest in the project had dried up and McDonnell Douglas pressed on with the new turbo fan-powered MD-90 series.

MD-11 PH-MCS of Martinair at Schiphol on 6 March 1996. The MD-11 was derived from the DC-10, retaining most of the latter's airframe but introducing several major new design features including all-new wings, a lengthened fuselage and more advanced engines. The first MD-11 (N111MD) was flown on 10 January 1990.

MD-11 HB-IWG of Swissair pictured at Zurich on 10 May 1997.

MD-11s have proved very popular with freighters. Pictured at Schiphol on 6 March 1996 is N274WA, owned by World Airways and leased to Malaysian Airline System.

On 29 August 1981 McDonnell Douglas was announced as the selected contractor for a long-range cargo aircraft for the USAF, following its C-X competition. Then, in January 1982, the Air Force said that it was not going to proceed with full-scale development. Finally, on 31 December 1985, a full-scale development contract for one flying prototype and two structural-test aircraft was awarded. The C-17A Globemaster III made its first flight on 15 September 1991. Pictured is a C-17A of the 437th Airlift Wing, AMC (Air Mobility Command), which began initial operations at Charleston AFB, South Carolina, in June 1993. To date, 120 C-17As have been approved to the year 2004.

In December 1983 the McDonnell Douglas Corporation announced that it was purchasing Hughes Helicopters, Inc. from the Howard Hughes estate. The sale was finalized on 6 January 1984 and on 27 August 1985 the company became the McDonnell Douglas Helicopter Company (MDHC). One of the designs acquired in the move was the AH-64D Longbow Apache, in production at a new plant at Falcon Field, Mesa, Arizona. From the seventy-first Apache onwards, in October 1985, the manufacturer's name was changed officially to McDonnell Douglas. A total of 232 AH-64Ds are on order for the US Army and thirty are being built for the Royal Netherlands Air Force. In July 1995 the MoD announced that Britain would purchase sixty-seven MD/GKN Westland-built WAH-64 Apaches for the Army Air Corps.